SMOKING FISH

IRRESISTIBLE RECIPES FOR SMOKED FISH TUNA, TROUT, SALMON AND OTHER FISH

BY RACHEL MILLS

TABLE OF CONTENTS

INTRODUCTION

Smoking fish or grilling it is not only a means of cooking but this is a form of Art or a form of Lifestyle! Smoking is something has withstood the test of time, it will continue to stand the test of time for years to come. Not only is it a method to preserve your catch or kill, but it's also one of if not the best-tasting food there is. This is an ultimate how-to guide for smoking all types of fish.

This book on smoking fish for beginners is the guide to mastering the low and slow art of smoking tuna, trout, salmon, and other fish at your home. This guide is an essential book for beginners who want to smoke fish without needing expert help from others. This book offers detailed guidance obtained by years of smoking meat, includes clear instructions and step-by-step directions for every recipe. This is the only guide you will ever need to professionally smoke a variety of fish. The book includes from well-known ALDER PLANK SMOKED TUNA to APPLE SMOKED SALMON STEAKS smoked fish recipes. Whether you are a beginner fish smoker or looking to go beyond the basics, the book gives you the tools and tips you need to start that perfectly smoked fish.

CHAPTER-1 TROUT RECIPES

TENDER SMOKED TROUT

TOTAL COOKING & PREPARATION TIME: 4 HOURS 15 MINUTES
TOTAL SERVINGS: ABOUT 2

INGREDIENTS

- 4-6 trout fillets
- ¼ cup soy sauce
- 2 cup water
- ½ Tbsp. salt
- ¼ cup teriyaki sauce
- 1 garlic clove, minced
- 1 tsp. lemon pepper
- 1 tsp. Celery seeds
- 1 tsp. salt
- Apple wood chips

COOKING DIRECTIONS

1. Mix soy sauce together with lemon pepper, garlic, teriyaki sauce, celery seeds and salt in a large bowl.

2. Place the fillets in the marinade and let marinade with the mixture and put in a refrigerator for overnight.

3. Next morning, transfer the fillets into a preheated smoker (212F, 100C).

4. Smoke the fillets for about 2 hours, then flip over and smoke for another 2 hours until the fish is flaky and dry, serve once done.

NUTRITION FACTS (ESTIMATED AMOUNT PER SERVING)

365 Calories
14.2g Total Fat
2.1g Saturated Fat
0g Trans Fat
92mg Cholesterol
5020mg Sodium
811mg Potassium
20.3g Carbohydrates
1.9g Dietary Fiber
11.5g Sugars
37.7g Protein

Salty Smoked Trouts with Dill Seeds

Total Cooking & Preparation time: 4 hours 15 minutes
Total Servings: About 2

Ingredients

- 5-6 trout fillets, with skin
- Ground black pepper as per taste
- 1 tsp. dry oregano
- 1 tsp. Salt
- 1/2 cup dry cherry chips

Cooking Directions

1. Preheat your smoker for 8 to 10 minutes until the smoke turns into light strands.
2. Place trout fillets on a dish and sprinkle with salt and black pepper.
3. Place the fillets with on the smoker (preferably skin side down) and smoke for an hour or two.
4. Flip & smoke the other side of the fish until it gets the flaky texture.

5. Once cooked, peel off the skin from the fillets, season with oregano and serve.

Nutrition Facts (Estimated Amount Per Serving)

297 Calories
13.2g Total Fat
2.3g Saturated Fat
0g Trans Fat
115mg Cholesterol
1267mg Sodium
731mg Potassium
0.5g Carbohydrates
0.3g Dietary Fiber
0g Sugars
41.4g Protein

HICKORY PLANK SMOKED TROUTS

TOTAL COOKING & PREPARATION TIME: 4 HOURS 30 MINUTES
TOTAL SERVINGS: ABOUT 6

INGREDIENTS

- 3-4 trout fillets, without skin
- 2 Tbsp. lime zest
- 4 Tbsp. Virgin olive oil
- 2 Tsp. salt
- 1 sprig of seaweed
- 1 sliced lemon
- 2 Tbsp. sugar
- 4 garlic cloves, finely chopped
- 2 hickory planks
- Applewood chips

COOKING DIRECTIONS

1. Mix brown sugar together with olive oil, lemon zest, garlic, and salt in a large bowl.
2. Marinate the fillets with the above mixture and refrigerate for overnight.

3. Soak wood chips and hickory plank in water for about an hour.

4. Preheat the smoker (212F, 100C) and place the fillets along with seaweed and slices of lemon.

5. Smoke the fillets for about 3 hours until dry and flaky, serve.

NUTRITION FACTS (ESTIMATED AMOUNT PER SERVING)

372 Calories
26.7g Total Fat
5.3g Saturated Fat
0g Trans Fat
53mg Cholesterol
1398mg Sodium
30mg Potassium
14.3g Carbohydrates
2.5g Dietary Fiber
5.9g Sugars
20.3g Protein

SMOKED TROUTS WITH ORANGE & BASIL

INGREDIENTS

- 1 Orange zest, grated
- 6 lb (2,7kg) ground trout
- 1/2 cup fresh oregano
- 1/2 cup Kosher salt
- Apple wood chips

COOKING DIRECTIONS

1. Butterfly the fish and remove insides.
2. Mix oregano with orange zest in a dish.
3. Apply salt on the trout on both the sides.
4. Sprinkle oregano in the inside of the fish and refrigerate for overnight.
5. Next morning, wash off the salt on the trout and refrigerate for a day.
6. Place the trout on a preheated smoker for 3-4 hours, serve.

NUTRITION FACTS (ESTIMATED AMOUNT PER SERVING)

265 Calories
10.2g Total Fat
2.9g Saturated Fat
0g Trans Fat
87mg Cholesterol
14202mg Sodium
763mg Potassium
11.4g Carbohydrates
6.2g Dietary Fiber
0.4g Sugars

SPICY SMOKED TROUTS

TOTAL COOKING & PREPARATION TIME: 3 HOURS AND 30 MINUTES
TOTAL SERVINGS: ABOUT 10

INGREDIENTS

- 6 lbs (2,7kgs) trout
- 1/2 cup white sugar
- 1/2 cup brown sugar
- 1 Tbsp. Kosher salt
- 1 Tbsp. smoked paprika
- 1 Tbsp. ground ginger powder
- 4 garlic cloves, minced
- 1 Tbsp. chili powder
- 1 Tbsp. onion powder
- 1 tsp. cumin
- 1 tsp. mustard powder
- 1 Tbsp. dried oregano, powdered
- 1/2 tsp. cayenne pepper
- 1 Tbsp. dried basil
- 1 tsp. ground black pepper
- Wood chips or chunks

COOKING DIRECTIONS

1. Mix brown sugar together with paprika, white sugar, kosher salt, smoked paprika, garlic powder, ginger powder, mustard powder, cumin, cayenne pepper, black pepper and oregano in a large bowl.

2. Marinate the fish with the above mixture, both on the inside and outside.

3. Refrigerate the marinated fish for about 3-4 hours or overnight.

4. Soak the wood chips for about an hour and preheat the smoker.

5. Smoke the fish for 2-3 hours until flaky, serve.

NUTRITION FACTS (ESTIMATED AMOUNT PER SERVING)

596 Calories
23.5g Total Fat
4.1g Saturated Fat
0g Trans Fat
201mg Cholesterol
891mg Sodium
1331mg Potassium
19.8g Carbohydrates
0.9g Dietary Fiber
17.5g Sugars
73g Protein

Smoked Trouts with Lime

Total Cooking & Preparation time: Approximately 1 hour
Total Servings: About 6

Ingredients

- 4 lb (1,8kg) trout
- 2 limes, sliced into halved
- 1 tsp. ground pepper
- 1 tsp. Salt
- Hardwood chips

Cooking Directions

1. Soak the wood chips in water for an hour.

2. Sprinkle salt and ground pepper on the inside and outside of the trout.

3. Preheat the smoker, setting it for indirect smoking.

4. Smoke each side of the fish for about 15-20 minutes until the fish is non-transparent.

5. Serve with lime slices.

NUTRITION FACTS (ESTIMATED AMOUNT PER SERVING)

582 Calories
25.7g Total Fat
4.5g Saturated Fat
0g Trans Fat
224mg Cholesterol
591mg Sodium
1427mg Potassium
2.6g Carbohydrates
0.7g Dietary Fiber
0.4g Sugars
80.7g Protein

Pepper-Glazed Smoked Trout

Total Cooking & Preparation time: 1 hour
Total Servings: About 12

Ingredients

- 1 whole golden trout (About 5 kgs,11 lbs)
- 2 Tbsp. dried basil
- 1 cup hot pepper jelly
- 1 cup apple cider lemon herb brine
- Green salad to serve

Cooking Directions

1. Clean the fish; remove the insides.

2. Add the brine and half cup of hot pepper jelly to the trout.

3. Place the fish in a medium sized zip lock bag and refrigerate overnight.

4. Put dried basil on the preheated smoker.

5. Glaze the trout with ½ cup of hot pepper jelly.

6. Smoke the fish for about 25-30 minutes on medium heat settings.

7. Serve with green salad.

NUTRITION FACTS (ESTIMATED AMOUNT PER SERVING)

771 Calories
47.5g Total Fat
7.9g Saturated Fat
0g Trans Fat
258mg Cholesterol
1718mg Sodium
1mg Potassium
14.5g Carbohydrates
0g Dietary Fiber
13.2g Sugars
79.2g Protein

Easy Smoked Trout

Total Cooking & Preparation time: 1 hour
Total Servings: About 6

Ingredients

- 1 lb (450g) trout fillets, with skin
- 2 cups water
- 1 cup dark brown sugar
- ½ cup coarse salt
- 1 Tbsp. Vegetable oil, for grill basket
- Cherry wood chips

Cooking Directions

1. Prepare the brine with sugar, salt, and water.

2. Place the fish in a zip lock bag with the brine and refrigerate for about 2 hours.

3. Pre soak the cherry wood chips and place them on the smoker.

4. Preheat the smoker for indirect smoking and medium heat settings.

5. Smoke each side of the fish for about 10-12 minutes and serve hot.

Nutrition Facts (Estimated Amount Per Serving)

383 Calories
13g Total Fat
2.3g Saturated Fat
0g Trans Fat
84mg Cholesterol
11610mg Sodium
574mg Potassium
35.6g Carbohydrates
0g Dietary Fiber
35.2g Sugars
30.2g Protein

Black Pepper Smoked Trout

Total Cooking & Preparation time: 3 hours 30 minutes
Total Servings: About 12

Ingredients

- 1 whole rainbow trout, with skin (About 5 kgs, 11 lbs)
- 1 tsp. lime juice
- 1 sliced lime
- 1 Tbsp. garlic salt
- 2 Tbsp. soy sauce
- 1 tsp. black pepper
- 1 tsp. smoked paprika
- Wood chips as per choice

Cooking Directions

1. Prepare a mixture of lime juice, soy sauce, garlic salt, smoked paprika and black pepper.
2. Marinate the fish on the inside as well as outside with the marinade.
3. Refrigerate the fish for 3-4 hours.

4. Place the fish on a pre heated smoker for about 3 hours.

5. Place the sliced lime over the fish while smoking.

6. Once the fish has a dry and flaky texture, remove and serve.

NUTRITION FACTS (ESTIMATED AMOUNT PER SERVING)

641 Calories
28.3g Total Fat
4.9g Saturated Fat
0g Trans Fat
247mg Cholesterol
374mg Sodium
1572mg Potassium
1.8g Carbohydrates
0.4g Dietary Fiber
0.4g Sugars
89.2g Protein

Tea-Smoked Trout with Salad

Total Cooking & Preparation time: 45 minutes
Total Servings: About 4

Ingredients

- 12 ounces (350g) trout
- 1 tsp. Dijon mustard
- 1 lb (450g) potatoes, sliced to half
- 1 Tbsp. white wine vinegar
- 2 Tbsp. virgin olive oil
- 1 tsp. Dry basil
- 10 tea bags, non-herbal
- 4 medium-sized onions, sliced
- 1/2 cup long-grain rice
- ¼ cup Demerara sugar

Cooking Directions

1. Boil the potatoes for 12-15 minutes in salted water and slice them into halves.

2. Prepare a mixture of olive oil, mustard, dry basil and wine vinegar.

3. Slice onions and add to the dressing along with boiled potatoes.

4. Prepare and wrap the mixture of rice, sugar and tea leaves and make small holes.

5. Place the above-made foil in the pre heated smoker.

6. Put the trout on the smoker and cook for about 20-25 minutes until the fish is flakey.

7. Serve with salad.

NUTRITION FACTS (ESTIMATED AMOUNT PER SERVING)

464 Calories
14.6g Total Fat
2.3g Saturated Fat
0g Trans Fat
63mg Cholesterol
86mg Sodium
1109mg Potassium
55.6g Carbohydrates
5.4g Dietary Fiber
14.8g Sugars
27.5g Protein

CHAPTER-2 TUNA RECIPES

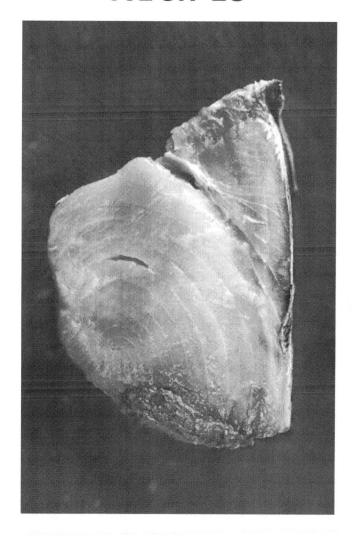

Simple Smoked Tuna

Total Cooking & Preparation time: Approximately 5 hours
Total Servings: About 10

Ingredients

- 10 lbs (4,5kgs) tuna fillets, sliced into 1-2 inch pieces
- 1 cup brown sugar, packed with a quart warm water
- 1 cup Kosher salt
- 4 bay leaves, finely crushed
- 1/2 ounce (14g) ground black pepper
- Maple wood chips

Cooking Directions

1. Pre-soak the maple wood chips for an hour and let it dry.

2. Prepare a mixture of salt, sugar and black pepper in warm water, add bay leaves.

3. Slice tuna in half an inch' pieces, however, do not peel off the skin.

4. Put the fish in the water mixture and let soak for approximately 2 hours.

5. Let the fillets dry in a cool place overnight so that the pellicle is formed.

6. Smoke the fillets for around 9-10 hours at a temperature of 120-140F (50-60C)

7. Raise the temperature to around 200F (90C) and smoke the fillets for 1 hour, flip over and smoke the other side for about an hour, serve.

NUTRITION FACTS (ESTIMATED AMOUNT PER SERVING)

731 Calories
58.2g Total Fat
0g Saturated Fat
0g Trans Fat
0mg Cholesterol
9434mg Sodium
36mg Potassium
13.1g Carbohydrates
0.5g Dietary Fiber
11.7g Sugars
39.6g Protein

SMOKED TUNA IN WINE

TOTAL COOKING & PREPARATION TIME: ABOUT 9 HOURS
TOTAL SERVINGS: ABOUT 8

INGREDIENTS

- 8-10 lbs (3,6-4,5kgs)Tuna fish
- ¼ cup unionized salt
- ⅓ cup brown sugar
- 1 cup water
- 2 cups coconut amino's
- ½ tsp. garlic powder
- ½ tsp. onion powder
- ½ tsp. red hot pepper sauce
- ½ tsp. black pepper
- 1 cup white wine, dry
- Wood chips of choice

COOKING DIRECTIONS

1. Prepare a mixture of salt, brown sugar, coconut amino, garlic powder, onion powder, pepper sauce, black pepper and white wine, ensuring sugar and salt get completely dissolved.

2. Cut the fish into small pieces and immerse in the brine prepared above, refrigerate for 8 hours or overnight.

3. Set the smoker on low heat settings and smoke the fish for about 4 hours.

4. Flip over the fish and smoke on low heat settings for another 4 hours until the dryness is achieved and the texture looks flaky.

5. Season as per taste and serve with green salad.

NUTRITION FACTS (ESTIMATED AMOUNT PER SERVING)

652 Calories
13.4g Total Fat
3.6g Saturated Fat
0g Trans Fat
189mg Cholesterol
8838mg Sodium
1211mg Potassium
13.5g Carbohydrates
0.6g Dietary Fiber
9.5g Sugars
110.4g Protein

Smoked Tuna Steaks in Peppercorns

Total Cooking & Preparation time: 7 hours 20 minutes
Total Servings: About 8

Ingredients

- 5 pcs of 10-ounce (280g) tuna steaks
- 2/3 cup unionized salt
- 2 quarts water
- 5 bay leaves
- 1/2 cup brown sugar
- 2 Tbsp. Vegetable oil
- 2 Tbsp. lime zest
- 4 cups white wine, dry
- 2 Tbsp. black peppercorns, grounded
- Apple wood chunks

Cooking Directions

1. Pre soak the apple wood chips for about an hour.

2. Prepare a mixture of salt, lime zest, brown sugar and bay leave to make a brine.

3. Place the tuna steaks along with the brine in a zip lock bag.

4. Refrigerate the bag for about 3 hours, turning the bag a couple of times.

5. Take the steaks off the bag, rinse with water and let it dry for 30 minutes to an hour so a pellicle is formed.

6. Apply oil on both the sides of the fish and sprinkle black peppercorns.

7. Pre heats the smoker in medium heat settings.

8. Add dry white wine to a water pan and place it on the smoker.

9. Smoke the steaks for 2 hours, flip over and smoke the other side for 2 hours until the fish turns flaky.

NUTRITION FACTS (ESTIMATED AMOUNT PER SERVING)

364 Calories
5.1g Total Fat
1.1g Saturated Fat
0g Trans Fat
82mg Cholesterol
3771mg Sodium
976mg Potassium
13.7g Carbohydrates
0.7g Dietary Fiber
9.8g Sugars
43.8g Protein

Smoked Tuna Fillets with Champagne

Total Cooking & Preparation time: Approximately 3 hours
Total Servings: About 4

Ingredients

- 12-15 lbs (5,4-6,8kgs) tuna fillets, sliced into 1/2 inch pieces
- 2 cups water
- 2 cups champagne of choice
- 2 Tbsp. white Worcestershire sauce
- 2 bottles of teriyaki glaze
- Juice of 1 lemon
- 1 Tbsp. Red hot pepper sauce
- 2 cups brown sugar
- 1 Tbsp. Lime zest
- 2 Tbsp. black pepper
- 1 Tbsp. onion salt
- 1 Tbsp. white pepper
- 1 Tbsp. garlic salt
- 1 tsp. red pepper
- Wood chunks of choice

Cooking Directions

1. Pre soak the wood chunks for about an hour
2. Pre heat the smoker on medium heat settings and fill the pan with champagne and water
3. Prepare a wet mixture of teriyaki glaze, red hot pepper sauce, lime zest, lemon juice and Worcestershire sauce
4. Slice the fillets into half inch pieces
5. Prepare a dry mixture of red, white, black pepper, garlic and onion salt
6. Place the fillets on wet mixture and later coat the fillets with dry mixture
7. Put the fillets on smoker and smoke for complete 2 hours (moist) or 3 hours (dry)
8. Add water and champagne to the pan if required

Nutrition Facts (Estimated Amount Per Serving)

1065 Calories
78g Total Fat
0.2g Saturated Fat
0g Trans Fat
4mg Cholesterol
464mg Sodium
170mg Potassium
37.2g Carbohydrates
1.2g Dietary Fiber
28.8g Sugars
55.7g Protein

Honey Smoked Tuna Steaks

Total Cooking & Preparation time: 6 hours 30 minutes
Total Servings: About 6

Ingredients

- 4 tuna steaks, about an inch thick
- 3/8 cup kosher salt
- 1 cup sugar
- ¼ tsp. garlic
- 1 tsp. black pepper
- 1 cup honey
- ¼ tsp. Prague powder
- 1-gallon water
- Cherry wood chips

Cooking Directions

1. Prepare a brine of salt, sugar, Prague powder, garlic, pepper, and honey in water.

2. Immerse tuna steaks in the brine and refrigerate overnight.

3. Preheat the smoker to 140F (60C).

4. Remove the steaks from the brine, dry them and place on the smoker.

5. Smoke for 3 hours, flip over and smoke for another 3 hours in order to achieve dry, flaky texture.

NUTRITION FACTS (ESTIMATED AMOUNT PER SERVING)

760 Calories
10.7g Total Fat
2.8g Saturated Fat
0g Trans Fat
83mg Cholesterol
10729mg Sodium
612mg Potassium
120.2g Carbohydrates
0.3g Dietary Fiber
119.6g Sugars
51.2g Protein

Smokey Yellow Tuna Dip

INGREDIENTS

- 2.5 lbs (1,1kgs) yellowfin tuna, cut into steaks
- ½ cup Kosher salt
- Warm water (for covering fillets)
- ½ cup mayonnaise
- 1/4 cup soy sauce, reduced sodium
- 1/3 cup diced red onion,
- 8 oz. (226g) whipping cream cheese
- 1 Tbsp. lime juice
- ¼ cup chopped Chervil
- ½ tsp. black pepper
- 2 minced garlic cloves
- ½ Tbsp. hot sauce
- Wood chips of choice

COOKING DIRECTIONS

1. Dissolve kosher salt in water to prepare the brine.

2. Immerse the steaks in the brine and refrigerate overnight.

3. Rinses the steaks with cold water and dry them.

4. Brush the steaks with soy sauce on both sides.

5. Preheat the smoker at 250F (120C) and smoke the steaks for about an hour.

6. Prepare a mixture of mayonnaise and whipping cheese.

7. Chop garlic, onions, and chervils and add it to the mixture of cheese and mayonnaise.

8. Add lime juice, hot sauce, salt, and pepper to the mixture and mix them well.

9. Dip the smoked steaks into the above-prepared mixture and refrigerate for 30 minutes.

10. Serve with pita or toasted bread.

NUTRITION FACTS (ESTIMATED AMOUNT PER SERVING)

542 Calories
21.7g Total Fat
5.6g Saturated Fat
4.5g Trans Fat
68mg Cholesterol
7847mg Sodium
1149mg Potassium
55g Carbohydrates
1.3g Dietary Fiber
40.4g Sugars
36.1g Protein

LIME & LEMONY SMOKED TUNA

TOTAL COOKING & PREPARATION TIME: APPROXIMATELY 1 HOUR
TOTAL SERVINGS: ABOUT 8

INGREDIENTS

- 4 tuna fillets
- 2 pcs fresh lemons
- 1⁄4 tsp. salt
- 4 Tbsp. Lime juice
- 1 Tbsp. mustard
- 6 garlic cloves, minced
- 1⁄4 tsp. pepper
- 1 1⁄2 cup butter
- Alder wood chunks, pre-soaked

COOKING DIRECTIONS

1. Soak the wood chunks in water for an hour.

2. Preheat the smoker to 300F (150C)

3. Squeeze the juice of lemons, mix it with lime juice.

4. Add garlic, butter, salt, pepper, and mustard to the citrus juice and mix well in a bowl.

5. Add melted butter to the bowl and mix well.

6. Immerse the fillets in the above mixture of lemon, butter, and other ingredients.

7. Place the fillets on the smoker skin side down and pour over the remaining mixture.

8. Smoke for 20 minutes, then toss over and smoke for another 20 minutes.

9. Remove once the desired flaky and dry texture is achieved, serve.

NUTRITION FACTS (ESTIMATED AMOUNT PER SERVING)

506 Calories
50.5g Total Fat
21.9g Saturated Fat
0g Trans Fat
92mg Cholesterol
320mg Sodium
75mg Potassium
4.5g Carbohydrates
0.8g Dietary Fiber
0.9g Sugars
11.6g Protein

Spicy Smoked Tuna with Apple Juice

Total Cooking & Preparation time: 2 hours and 30 minutes
Total Servings: About 12

Ingredients

- 10 lbs (4,5kgs) tuna
- 2 1/2 cups apple juice
- 2 cups water
- 1/2 cup honey
- 2 cups brown sugar, firmly packed
- ½ cup unionized salt
- ½ cup coconut Aminos
- 1/8 cup Chinese chili sauce
- 1/8 cup molasses
- 3-4 bay leaves

Cooking Directions

1. Prepare a mixture of honey, sugar, apple juice, salt, coconut amino, chili sauce and bay leaves.

2. Heat the mixture in a pan until the salt is completely dissolved.

3. Slice tuna into 1 - 1 ½ inches chunks.

4. Immerse the chunks in the above-prepared brine and refrigerate overnight.

5. Remove the chunks, dry them and place in a cool, breezy place so that the pellicle is formed.

6. Preheat the smoker at 175F (80C) and place tuna chunks above it.

7. Smoke the chunks for an hour flip over and smoke for another one hour until the fish is flaky.

8. Remove the chunks from the smoker and serve.

NUTRITION FACTS (ESTIMATED AMOUNT PER SERVING)

887 Calories
30.6g Total Fat
6.3g Saturated Fat
0g Trans Fat
117mg Cholesterol
2247mg Sodium
1405mg Potassium
46.8g Carbohydrates
0.2g Dietary Fiber
42g Sugars
100.4g Protein

Smoked Tuna Steaks with Soy Sauce

Total Cooking & Preparation time: 1 hour 45 minutes
Total Servings: About 4

Ingredients

- 4 tuna steaks
- 2 tsp. kosher salt
- 1 Tbsp. Muscovado sugar
- 2-3 bay leaves
- 1 tsp. peppercorns
- 1 tsp. of Lea and Perrins sauce
- 1 Tbsp. soy sauce
- 2 cups water

Cooking Directions

1. Prepare a brine of kosher salt, sugar, bay leaves, peppercorns, Lea and Perrins sauce and soy sauce.

2. Add the steaks to the brine and refrigerate them overnight or for a minimum of 6 hours.

3. Remove the steaks and let them dry in a breezy place for about an hour to form a pellicle.

4. Place the steaks in a pre heated smoker, smoke each side for 12-15 minutes.

NUTRITION FACTS (ESTIMATED AMOUNT PER SERVING)

324 Calories
10.7g Total Fat
2.8g Saturated Fat
0g Trans Fat
83mg Cholesterol
1502mg Sodium
567mg Potassium
2.7g Carbohydrates
0.3g Dietary Fiber
1.9g Sugars
51.2g Protein

ALDER PLANK SMOKED TUNA

TOTAL COOKING & PREPARATION TIME: 2 HOURS 30 MINUTES
TOTAL SERVINGS: ABOUT 2

INGREDIENTS

- 3-4 tuna steaks
- 1 tsp. dried oregano
- 1/2 tsp. garlic salt
- 2 Tbsp. teriyaki sauce
- 1 box spinach, frozen
- 1 Tbsp. Lemon zest
- 2 Tbsp. coconut aminos
- 2 Tbsp. sesame seeds
- Apple or Cherry Wood chips
- 1 alder plank

COOKING DIRECTIONS

1. Pre-soak alder plank and wood chips for an hour.

2. Prepare a mixture of lemon zest, garlic salt, and dried oregano, apply the mixture on both sides of the steak and refrigerate overnight.

3. Mix teriyaki sauce, coconut amino's and sesame seeds in a bowl and apply the paste on the steak and place them on the alder plank.

4. Prepare around 10 small balls of frozen spinach and place them on the outside of the alder plank.

5. Place the plank on the smoker for a maximum of 1 ½ hours.

6. Once prepared, serve tuna steaks with spinach balls.

NUTRITION FACTS (ESTIMATED AMOUNT PER SERVING)

430 Calories
15.8g Total Fat
3.5g Saturated Fat
0g Trans Fat
83mg Cholesterol
900mg Sodium
1453mg Potassium
13.7g Carbohydrates
4.8g Dietary Fiber
3.5g Sugars
57.9g Protein

CHAPTER-3 SALMON RECIPES

Delicious Smoked Salmon

Total Preparation & Cooking Time: 30 hours
Total Servings: 20

Ingredients

- 1 cup kosher salt
- 1/2 cup sugar
- 1/2 cup dark brown sugar
- 1 tbsp. crushed black peppercorns
- 2 large salmon fillets or sides, pin bones removed

Cooking Directions

1. Mix sugar together with salt, peppercorns and brown sugar in a large bowl.

2. Spread a large size aluminum foil and top the foil with an equally long layer of a plastic wrap.

3. Sprinkle approximately 1/3 of the rub mixture onto the plastic wrap. Lay 1 side of the fish onto the rub (preferably skin down). Now, sprinkle approximately 1/3 of the rub over the flesh. Arrange the second side of the salmon onto the

first side (flesh size down). Use the leftover rub and cover the skin.

4. Fold the plastic wrap over to cover and then close the edges of foil; crimping tightly around the fish. Now, place the wrapped fish onto a sheet pan or plank and top with one more sheet pan or plank.

5. Weigh with a heavy brick or phone book and let refrigerate for overnight. Flip the fish over & refrigerate for 10 to 12 more hours.

6. Unwrap the fish; rinse the cure off using cold water. Pat the salmon dry with paper towels and then place them in a dry, cool place (not inside the fridge) for a couple of hours until the surface turns out to be dry. To speed up the process, you can use a fan.

7. Smoke the fish over smoldering sawdust or hardwood chips until a meat thermometer reflects 150F (65C); ensure you keep the smoker's temperature between 150 F (65C) to 160 F (70C).

NUTRITIONAL VALUE (ESTIMATED AMOUNT PER SERVING)

504 Calories
22g Total Fat
3.1g Saturated Fat
0g Trans Fat
157mg Cholesterol
5817mg Sodium
1377mg Potassium
8.8g Carbohydrates
0.1g Dietary Fiber
8.5g Sugars
69.1g Protein

QUICK & EASY SMOKED SALMON

TOTAL PREPARATION & COOKING TIME: 3 HOURS & 25 MINUTES
TOTAL SERVINGS: 06

INGREDIENTS

- 1-1/2 to 2 lb (0.7 to 1kg). salmon
- 1 Tbsp. black pepper
- 1/2 cup coarse salt
- 1 cup brown sugar
- 1 cup vodka

COOKING DIRECTIONS

1. Whisk brown sugar together with Vodka, pepper, and salt in a large bowl. Place the Salmon in a re-sealable bag, preferably large size. Transfer the marinade to the bag & massage the salmon with the marinade using your hands.

2. Refrigerate for a couple of hours. Remove the pieces from bag and place them on paper towels to dry.

3. Now, heat your smoker and smoke the salmon for half an hour (Skin-Side down) and with the lid open.

4. Increase the temperature to 230F (110C) & cook for 45 to 55 more minutes.

5. Refrigerate until ready to serve. Garnish with capers and lemons, if desired.

NUTRITIONAL VALUE (ESTIMATED AMOUNT PER SERVING)

280 Calories
4.7g Total Fat
0.7g Saturated Fat
0g Trans Fat
33mg Cholesterol
7721mg Sodium
336mg Potassium
24.4g Carbohydrates
0.3g Dietary Fiber
23.5g Sugars
14.8g Protein

Mouthwatering Smoked Salmon

Total Preparation & Cooking Time: 3 Hours & 15 Minutes
Total Servings: 4

Ingredients

- 1/3 cup sugar
- 3 -4 pounds (1,3-1,8kg) salmon fillets (with skin)
- 1/2 tsp. pepper
- 1 cup white wine, dry
- 1/2 tsp. garlic powder
- 1 cup water
- 1/2 tsp. onion powder
- 2 cups soy sauce
- 1/2 tsp. Tabasco sauce
- 1/4 cup salt, non-iodized

COOKING DIRECTIONS

1. Thoroughly mix all of the brine ingredients together in a large bowl.

2. Combine the salmon fillets with brine mixture in a large, deep pan and let soak for overnight, keeping refrigerated.

3. Thoroughly rinse the fillets after brining.

4. Using a paper towel; pat them dry and let the air dry for a minimum period of an hour before you smoke the fish.

5. Lay the salmon fillets (skin side down) on the smoker rack.

6. Cook in the smoker for 3 to 5 hours, at 165 F (73C) or until cooked through.

NUTRITIONAL VALUE (ESTIMATED AMOUNT PER SERVING)

632 Calories
21.1g Total Fat
3g Saturated Fat
0g Trans Fat
150mg Cholesterol
12221mg Sodium
1653mg Potassium
28.6g Carbohydrates
1.1g Dietary Fiber
19.5g Sugars
74.2g Protein

Honey Smoked Salmon with Berries

Total Cooking & Preparation time: Approximately 2 hours
Total Servings: About 4

Ingredients

- 2 lbs (1kgs) salmon fillet
- ¾ cup honey
- 10 allspice berries
- 1-quart water
- ½ cup kosher salt
- 10 peppercorns
- 2 bay leafs
- ¼ cup lemon juice
- 4 ounces (113g) rum
- 10 cloves
- Maple Wood chips

COOKING DIRECTIONS

1. Prepare a mixture of allspice berries, honey, kosher salt, bay leafs, peppercorns, lemon juice, and clove.

2. Dip the fillets into the brine made above, fill them in a zip lock bag and refrigerate for about 3 hours.

3. Rinse the filet with water, pat dry and set in a breezy atmosphere for about an hour for the formation of the pellicle.

4. Preheat the smoker at 160F (70C) and smoke the fillets for about 45 minutes.

5. Flip the fillets and smoke for another 45 minutes and serve.

NUTRITION FACTS (ESTIMATED AMOUNT PER SERVING)

609 Calories
16.1g Total Fat
2.7g Saturated Fat
0g Trans Fat
100mg Cholesterol
14274mg Sodium
1099mg Potassium
63.9g Carbohydrates
4.4g Dietary Fiber
52.6g Sugars
45.3g Protein

Perfectly Smoked Salmon

Total Cooking & Preparation time: 4 hours 30 minutes
Total Servings: About 8

Ingredients

- 5 lbs (2,2kgs) salmon
- 1/3 cup Diamond Crystal Kosher salt
- 1-quart cool water
- 1/2 cup maple syrup
- 1 cup brown sugar
- Maple wood chips

Cooking Directions

1. Prepare the brine by mixing water, Kosher salt, maple syrup and brown sugar.

2. Cover the fish with the brine and put it in a zip lock bag, refrigerate overnight.

3. Remove the salmon next morning, pat it dry and leave at a cool and dry place for the formation of the pellicle.

4. Put fish in the smoker and gradually increase the temperature (120F, 50C for about 2 hours,

140F, 60C for about one more hour and finally 175F, 80C for the last hour).

5. Ensure basting the fish every hour with the maple syrup.

6. Serve as per individual preferences.

Nutrition Facts (Estimated Amount Per Serving)

457 Calories
17.5g Total Fat
2.5g Saturated Fat
0g Trans Fat
125mg Cholesterol
4975mg Sodium
1124mg Potassium
21.1g Carbohydrates
0g Dietary Fiber
20.6g Sugars
55g Protein

SMOKED SALMON FILLETS WITH WHISKEY

TOTAL COOKING & PREPARATION TIME: APPROXIMATELY 12 HOURS
TOTAL SERVINGS: 3

INGREDIENTS

- 1 salmon fillet
- 1½ cup Bourbon whiskey
- 1 quart distilled water
- 4 tsp. non-iodized salt
- ½ cup brown sugar
- 1 tsp. fresh ground black pepper
- 1 tsp. garlic powder
- Wood chips as per choice

COOKING DIRECTIONS

1. Prepare the brine with whiskey, brown sugar, salt, garlic powder and black pepper.

2. Cover the fish with the brine and put it in a zip lock bag, refrigerate overnight.

3. Remove the salmon next morning, pat it dry and leave at a cool and dry place for the formation of the pellicle.

4. Pre heats the smoker and cook for 10 to 12 hours between 100F (40C) to 150F (65C).

5. Ensure to change the wood chips at least 3 times before the dish is finally prepared (i.e. every 4 hours).

NUTRITION FACTS (ESTIMATED AMOUNT PER SERVING)

475 Calories
22g Total Fat
3.2g Saturated Fat
0g Trans Fat
157mg Cholesterol
4033mg Sodium
1382mg Potassium
0.9g Carbohydrates
0.2g Dietary Fiber
0.2g Sugars
69.3g Protein

Smoked Salmon Fillets Candy

Total Cooking & Preparation time: 6 hours 30 minutes
Total Servings: About 10

Ingredients

- 5 pounds (2,3kg) salmon fillets, skin-on
- 1 cup maple syrup
- 1 lb (450g) brown sugar
- 1 lb (450g) Kosher salt

Cooking Directions

1. Slice the salmon into 2-inch thick fillets.

2. Prepare the brine with brown sugar and maple syrup.

3. Paste the brine over the fillets and put them in a zip-lock bag, refrigerate for 3-4 hours.

4. Remove the salmon next morning, pat it dry and leave at a cool and dry place for about 2 hours for the formation of the pellicle.

5. Put fish in the smoker and gradually increase the temperature (180F, 80C to 225F, 110C), smoke the fish for about 4 -6 hours.

6. Ensure basting the fish every 2 hours with the maple syrup.

Nutrition Facts (Estimated Amount Per Serving)

555 Calories
14.1g Total Fat
2g Saturated Fat
0g Trans Fat
100mg Cholesterol
17696mg Sodium
999mg Potassium
65.6g Carbohydrates
0g Dietary Fiber
62.8g Sugars
44.1gProtein

Apple Smoked Salmon Steaks

Total Cooking & Preparation time: 2 hours 30 minutes
Total Servings: About 4

Ingredients

- 5-6 salmon steaks
- 2 Tbsp. lime juice
- Apple wood chips
- 2 Tbsp. olive oil
- 1 tsp. tarragon
- 1 Tbsp. brown sugar
- ½ tsp. salt

Cooking Directions

1. Prepare a mixture of olive oil, lime juice, tarragon sugar and salt, till the sugar is dissolved.

2. Place the salmon steaks in a large-sized dish and add the marinade.

3. Refrigerate the steak overnight

4. Place the steaks on the smoker for an hour, flip it over and smoke for another hour till the steaks are dry and flaky

5. Braze the steaks with the marinade a couple of times while smoking them

NUTRITION FACTS (ESTIMATED AMOUNT PER SERVING)

369 Calories
20.8g Total Fat
3g Saturated Fat
0g Trans Fat
98mg Cholesterol
390mg Sodium
887mg Potassium
4.1g Carbohydrates
0.1g Dietary Fiber
2.6g Sugars
43.3g Protein

Sweet Smoked Salmon Fillets

Total Cooking & Preparation time: Approximately 6 hours
Total Servings: About 6

Ingredients

- 3-4 lbs (1,3-1,8kgs) salmon fillets, large sized
- 1 cup brown sugar
- 1/2 cup white sugar
- 1 tsp. ground black pepper
- 1/2 cup un-iodized salt
- 1 Tbsp. garlic powder
- 1/4 cup red pepper
- 1 Tbsp. Jacobsen salt

Cooking Directions

1. Prepare a mixture of brown sugar, white sugar, black pepper, and salt.

2. In a tin foil, topped up with a plastic wrap, Spread 1/3 of the above-made mixture and place salmon fillets, skin side down. Spread 1/3 of the remaining mixture over the fillets.

3. Wrap both the foils and place a heavy object evenly on the fillets, refrigerate overnight.

4. Mix red pepper, garlic powder, Jacobson salt and brown sugar in a bowl.

5. Paste the mixture on the meat side of the fillets.

6. leave the fillets in a cool and dry place for an hour for the formation of the pellicle.

7. Pre heats the smoker at 150F (65C) and smoke the fillets for 2-3 hours until flaky and dry.

NUTRITION FACTS (ESTIMATED AMOUNT PER SERVING)

561 Calories
18.7g Total Fat
2.7g Saturated Fat
0g Trans Fat
133mg Cholesterol
5057mg Sodium
1222mg Potassium
42g Carbohydrates
0.3g Dietary Fiber
40.7g Sugars
59g Protein

Orange Glazed Salmon Fillets

Total Cooking & Preparation time: Approximately 3 hours
Total Servings: About 4

Ingredients

- 3 lb (1,3kg) salmon fillets, without skin
- 1 cup salt
- Hickory wood chunks
- 1-quart water
- ½ cup brown sugar
- ½ cup of orange juice
- 1 orange
- 1 lime juice
- 1 lemon zest
- 4 dashes Tabasco sauce
- ½ tsp. oregano, dried
- 1 tsp. corn starch
- 2 Tbsp. balsamic vinegar
- 1-pint beer
- 2 Tbsp. olive oil

COOKING DIRECTIONS

1. Pre soak wood chunks overnight.

2. Prepare the brine with sugar, salt and 5 cups of water, soak the fillets for 2 hours.

3. Grate the zest of orange, lime, lemon and add juices to prepare the glaze.

4. Add oregano and tobacco sauce to the glaze.

5. Place the glaze on heat and simmer down to ½ of its content.

6. Mix cornstarch and vinegar and add to the orange glaze mixture, stir until it is thick.

7. Remove, rinse the salmon and paste them with olive oil.

8. Brush the fillets with the orange glaze and place it on the rack.

9. In a pan, add a pint of beer with a quart of water, place it on the smoker; and heat up.

10. Place the fillets rack on the smoker and smoke on medium heat settings for about 30 minutes, then flip the fillets and smoke for 30 more minutes.

11. Increase the heat settings to high and smoke for 1 more hour, serve as desired.

Nutrition Facts (Estimated Amount Per Serving)

678 Calories
28.2g Total Fat
4g Saturated Fat
0g Trans Fat
150mg Cholesterol
28465mg Sodium
1558mg Potassium
33.8g Carbohydrates
1.7g Dietary Fiber
25.1g Sugars
67.4g Protein

Smoked Salmon Fillets with Lemon Juice

Total Cooking & Preparation time: 1 hour 30 minutes
Total Servings: About 4

Ingredients

- 2 lbs (1kgs) Salmon fillet
- 2 Tbsp. olive oil
- Applewood chips
- 1 lemon juice
- Salt and pepper as desired
- 1 Tbsp. black pepper
- 1 tsp. lemon zest
- ½ tsp. coarse salt
- 3 Tbsp. green capers

Cooking Directions

1. Pre-soak wood chips for an hour.

2. Sprinkle olive oil, pepper, and salt on the skin side of the fish and olive oil and pepper on the meat side.

3. Wrap the fish in an aluminum foil and refrigerate for 2 hours.

4. Smoke the fish at a temperature of 400F (200C) for 20 minutes, flip it over and another 20 minutes until the fish is flaky.

5. Mix a tbsp. of lemon zest along with the same amount of olive oil.

6. Crush a tsp. of caper and mix it with salt, add this to the mixture of olive oil and lemon zest to prepare the sauce.

7. Serve fish with sauce over it.

NUTRITION FACTS (ESTIMATED AMOUNT PER SERVING)

367 Calories
21.1g Total Fat
3.1g Saturated Fat
0g Trans Fat
100mg Cholesterol
343mg Sodium
907mg Potassium
1.4g Carbohydrates
0.5g Dietary Fiber
0.3g Sugars
44.3g Protein

CHAPTER-4 OTHER FISHES RECIPES

Smoked & Spicy Tilapia

Total Cooking & Preparation time: 1 hour 15 minutes
Total Servings: About 4

Ingredients

- 4 lbs (1,8kgs) tilapia fillets
- 2 Tbsp. red pepper flakes
- 2 Tbsp. melted butter
- 1 Tbsp. pepper
- 2 Tbsp. salt

Cooking Directions

1. Brush tilapia fillets with melted butter and sprinkle with fillets and pepper flakes.
2. Pre heats the smoker to 200F (90C) and smoke for an hour.
3. Remove the fillets when they are dry and flaky.

NUTRITION FACTS (ESTIMATED AMOUNT PER SERVING)

437 Calories
10.4g Total Fat
5.6g Saturated Fat
0g Trans Fat
236mg Cholesterol
3691mg Sodium
76mg Potassium
2.5g Carbohydrates
1.1g Dietary Fiber
0.3g Sugars
84.9g Protein

SMOKED SNAPPER WITH LEMONS

TOTAL COOKING & PREPARATION TIME: 45 MINUTES
TOTAL SERVINGS: 2

INGREDIENTS

- 2 snapper fillets
- 4 tsp. melted butter
- 3 large lemons
- 1 tsp. Canola oil spray
- 1 tsp. Smoked paprika
- 1 tsp. Dried basil

COOKING DIRECTIONS

1. Wash fillets under running cold water and pat dry them.

2. Cut lemons into thin slices and melt butter.

3. Pre heats the smoker at medium heat settings.

4. Oil one of the lemon sides and place them on the smoker.

5. Put the fillets on top of the slices; brush melted butter and sprinkle smoked paprika.

6. Smoke the fillets for 10 minutes, flip over and smoke for another 10 minutes until they turn nontransparent.

7. Garnish with basil and serve.

Nutrition Facts (Estimated Amount Per Serving)

206 Calories
9.5g Total Fat
4.9g Saturated Fat
0g Trans Fat
60mg Cholesterol
107mg Sodium
150mg Potassium
8.8g Carbohydrates
2.9g Dietary Fiber
2.3g Sugars
23.2g Protein

Easy Smoked Marlin

Total Cooking & Preparation time: 2 hours 30 minutes
Total Servings: About 8

Ingredients

- 10-ounce (280g) marlin steaks
- 3 quarters water
- 2 1/2 cups apple juice
- 1 cup soy sauce
- 1 cup brown sugar
- 1/4 cup Kosher salt
- 1 Tbsp. whole peppercorns
- 1 garlic clove minced
- 4-5 bay leaves
- Applewood chips

Cooking Directions

1. Prepare the brine by combining water, apple juice, kosher salt, sugar, peppercorns, garlic cloves and bay leaves.

2. Immerse the steaks into the brine and put it in a zip-lock bag, refrigerate overnight.

3. Preheat the smoker and set it up for indirect smoking.

4. Remove the fish from the brine, pat dry and place it on the smoker.

5. Smoke at a temperature of 200F (90C) for about an hour, flip over and another hour.

6. Serve with kebabs or rice.

NUTRITION FACTS (ESTIMATED AMOUNT PER SERVING)

585 Calories
18.2g Total Fat
0.1g Saturated Fat
0g Trans Fat
0mg Cholesterol
1806mg Sodium
186mg Potassium
30g Carbohydrates
0.7g Dietary Fiber
25.6g Sugars
71.3g Protein

Smoked Halibut with White Wine

Total Cooking & Preparation time: 1 hour 30 minutes
Total Servings: About 4

Ingredients

- 5 lbs (2,2kgs) halibut fillets
- 6 Tbsp. melted butter
- A dash of salt
- 2 garlic cloves, minced
- ½ cup white wine
- A dash of pepper
- Applewood chips

Cooking Directions

1. Melt butter and add salt, pepper, and minced garlic to it.

2. Put the fillets into the mixture and refrigerate for an hour.

3. Pre heats the smoker at 225F (110C) and put the fillets on the smoker.

4. Smoke for 30 minutes, flip over and another 30 minutes until the fish is dry and has achieved the flaky texture.

Nutrition Facts (Estimated Amount Per Serving)

577 Calories
25.7g Total Fat
12.1g Saturated Fat
0g Trans Fat
162mg Cholesterol
358mg Sodium
1674mg Potassium
1.3g Carbohydrates
0g Dietary Fiber
0.3g Sugars
75.9g Protein

ALDER SMOKED BLACK COD

TOTAL COOKING & PREPARATION TIME: APPROXIMATELY 3 HOURS
TOTAL SERVINGS: ABOUT 4

INGREDIENTS

- 3 lbs (1,3kgs) black cod fillets, with skin
- 1/4 cup sugar
- 1 Tbsp. Sweet paprika
- 2 Tbsp. Honey
- 1 cup Kosher salt
- Alder wood
- 2 Tbsp. garlic powder

COOKING DIRECTIONS

1. Prepare a mixture of salt, sugar and garlic powder in a dish.

2. Slice the fillets into the 1-inch size and place it into a plastic container, skin side down and refrigerate.

3. Remove the fillets from the container, rinse and pat dry.

4. Leave in a cool, breezy environment so that it can develop the pellicle.

5. Pre heats the smoker at 160F (70C) and smoke each side of the fish for an hour each.

6. Glaze the fillets with honey in every 30 minutes while the smoking process.

7. Sprinkle the fillets with sweet paprika and serve.

NUTRITION FACTS (ESTIMATED AMOUNT PER SERVING)

308 Calories
17.5g Total Fat
4.6g Saturated Fat
0.2g Trans Fat
53mg Cholesterol
28348mg Sodium
98mg Potassium
25.9g Carbohydrates
1.1g Dietary Fiber
22.3g Sugars
13.8g Protein

CONCLUSION

Thank you again for downloading this book! I hope this book was able to help you with the recipes that you can try while at home and can give your loved ones the proper diet that they deserve. The next step is to start trying these recipes and see a notice in their health. Finally, if you enjoyed this book, then I'd like to ask you for a favor, would you be kind enough to leave a review for this book on Amazon? It'd be greatly appreciated!

Thank you and good luck!

OTHER BOOKS BY
RACHEL MILLS

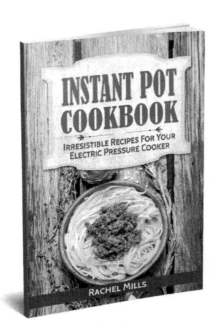

INSTANT POT COOKBOOK
IRRESISTIBLE RECIPES FOR YOUR
ELECTRIC PRESSURE COOKER

Amazon.com
https://www.amazon.com/dp/1548120413
CreateSpace eStore:
https://www.createspace.com/7259453

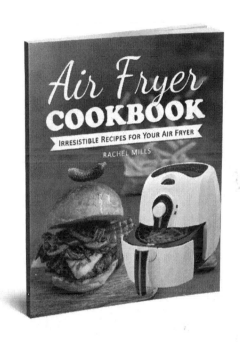

AIR FRYER COOKBOOK IRRESISTIBLE RECIPES FOR YOUR AIR FRYER

Amazon.com
https://www.amazon.com/dp/1974142949
CreateSpace eStore:
https://www.createspace.com/7416839

P.S. Thank you for reading this book. If you've enjoyed this book, please don't shy, drop me a line, leave a review or both. I love reading reviews and your opinion is extremely important for me.

My Page on Amazon
amazon.com/author/rachelmills

ISBN-13:978-1976011214

ISBN-10:1976011213

Disclaimer and Terms of Use:The effort has been made to ensure that the information in this book is accurate and complete, however, the author and the publisher do not warrant the accuracy of the information, text, and graphics contained within the book due to the rapidly changing nature of science, research, known and unknown facts and the internet. The Author and the publisher do not hold any responsibility for errors, omissions or contrary interpretation of the subject matter herein. This book is presented solely for motivational and informational purposes only.

Made in the USA
Middletown, DE
08 September 2019